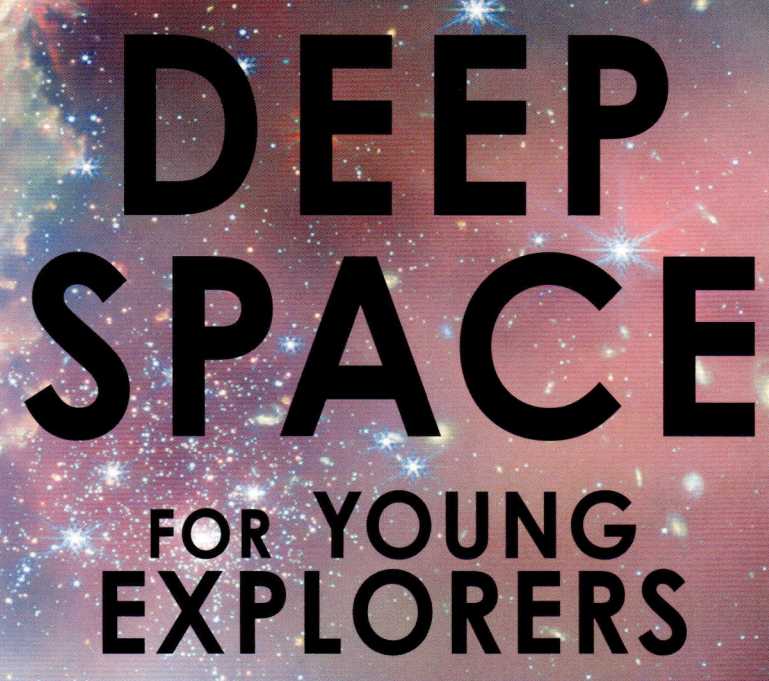

# DEEP SPACE
## FOR YOUNG EXPLORERS

By the astronomers of
Royal Observatory Greenwich

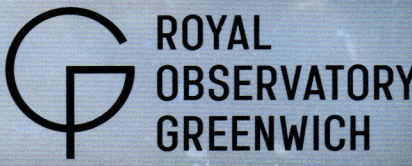

First published in Great Britain in 2026 by Wayland
Copyright © Hodder and Stoughton Ltd., 2026
All rights reserved

Editor: Grace Glendinning
Designer: Laura Hambleton
Contributors from the Astronomy team
at Royal Observatory Greenwich:
Imo Bell, Ed Bloomer, Greg Brown, Jake Foster,
Anna Gammon-Ross, Sam Imperato, Jessica Lee,
Catherine Muller, Tania de Sales Marques

HB ISBN: 978 1 5263 3073 4
PB ISBN: 978 1 5263 3075 8
Ebook ISBN: 978 1 5263 3074 1

Printed and bound in Dubai.

Wayland, an imprint of
Hachette Children's Group
Part of Hodder and Stoughton
Carmelite House
50 Victoria Embankment
London EC4Y 0DZ

An Hachette UK Company
www.hachette.co.uk
www.hachettechildrens.co.uk

MIX
Paper | Supporting
responsible forestry
FSC® C104740

The authorised representative in the EEA is
Hachette Ireland, 8 Castlecourt Centre, Dublin 15,
D15 XTP3, Ireland (email: info@hbgi.ie)

Photo credits: see page 63

We strongly advise that Internet access is supervised by a responsible adult. The website addresses (URLs) included in this book were valid at the time of going to press. However, it is possible that contents or addresses may have changed since the publication of this book. No responsibility for any such changes can be accepted by either the author or the Publisher.

# CONTENTS

| | |
|---|---|
| Foreword | 4 |
| Timeline of space photography | 6 |

## WAYS OF SEEING

| | |
|---|---|
| What is light? | 8 |
| Hubble and Webb: Two unique views | 10 |
| Improving with time: Pillars of Creation | 12 |
| Different instruments | 14 |
| Zooming in: The Horsehead Nebula | 16 |
| Zooming in: Andromeda Galaxy | 18 |

## STARS AND NEBULAE

| | |
|---|---|
| Our nearest star | 20 |
| Next-door star neighbour | 22 |
| Jewels in the sky | 24 |
| Stars forming on a grand scale | 26 |
| The local nursery | 28 |
| That's a lot: Inside a globular cluster | 30 |
| It's looking right at me! | 32 |
| Spot the difference | 34 |
| Don't fall in! | 36 |
| It's history! | 38 |
| Where does a zombie star come from? | 40 |

## GALAXIES

| | |
|---|---|
| The galactic zoo | 42 |
| The Milky Way | 44 |
| Our galactic neighbour | 46 |
| Galactic lookalike | 48 |
| Galactic crash | 50 |
| Clusters of clusters | 52 |
| HOW many? | 54 |

## DATA

| | |
|---|---|
| Mapping the neighbourhood | 56 |
| What about further out? | 58 |
| How far can we go? | 60 |
| Glossary, Quick quiz, Further information | 62 |
| Index and Answers | 64 |

# FOREWORD

It might sound silly, but one of the most important things to remember in astronomy is that your eyes are little optical instruments. They are amazing tools, but when you gaze into the night sky, you might feel overwhelmed by how much there is to take in. Not even the sharpest pair of eyes can capture everything at once.

Distant galaxies, colourful nebulae, star clusters and the glowing remains of supernova explosions are all out there, waiting to be explored. Some of these objects are too faint to spot without a telescope. Others shine brightly in forms our eyes can't detect. Your own view of space from Earth is packed with so much detail, and it can appear completely different depending on which type of telescope you use. To top it all off, you can spot new things each time you look up because deep space is always changing. (In this book, deep space means anything that lies outside our solar system.)

That's why the astronomers at Royal Observatory Greenwich made a plan. We wanted to share with you as many amazing objects from deep space as we could, to show you just how beautiful, strange and surprising the Universe can be. We also wanted to tell a bit of a story to show how astronomers piece together clues over time to build our view of the Universe. Each astronomer that helped with this book has included their own ideas about what the most interesting objects are, and we hope to inspire you to find your own favourite corners of space!

This is our attempt to fit the biggest possible view of the Universe into one book. While we think we have made some exciting choices, hopefully this is just the starting point for you to discover even more. After all, there is still so much Universe left to explore ...

Edward Bloomer
Royal Observatory Greenwich

NASA's James Webb Space Telescope released this image on 24 March 2025. It shows material flowing from a star as it is forming. Turn the page for even more cosmic beauty!

# TIMELINE OF SPACE PHOTOGRAPHY

✳

This book is filled with beautiful photographs of our Universe. But it has taken a lot of hard work and clever science to get us this far.

Let's look at some of the ground-breaking moments in humanity's quest to capture space in photos.

## 1959
### FIRST VIEW OF THE FAR SIDE OF THE MOON
From here on Earth, we always see the same side of the Moon, so this photo gave us a whole new view.

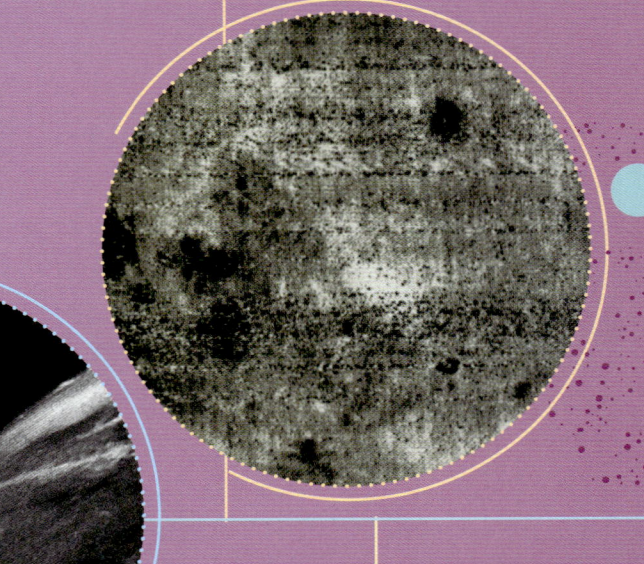

### FIRST SOLAR ECLIPSE PHOTOGRAPH
Julius Berkowski took this image at the Royal Observatory in Königsberg, Prussia (now Kaliningrad, Russia), showing the Moon blocking out his view of the Sun.

**1851**

### FIRST PHOTO OF EARTH FROM SPACE
The camera that took this picture actually fell back to Earth! Luckily, the film containing the photos survived.

**1946**

### FIRST COLOUR IMAGE OF EARTH FROM THE MOON
William Anders, part of the first crew to orbit the Moon, captured this on Christmas Eve.

**1968**

**1990**

**THE HUBBLE SPACE TELESCOPE'S FIRST IMAGE**

Being outside Earth's atmosphere gave the Hubble Space Telescope (Hubble) a clearer view of the Universe. The bright marks in each image are stars.

**2022**

**THE JAMES WEBB SPACE TELESCOPE'S FIRST IMAGES**

From its first picture to today, the James Webb Space Telescope (Webb) has given us some of the deepest views out into the Universe yet.

The same view photographed from Earth (a ground-based image) was much blurrier.

*This was only a very quick journey through more than a hundred years of photography. But with so much to see, it's time to start exploring space!*

# WHAT IS LIGHT?

It's important to first think about what we're looking at when we're looking at photos of space. Because most things in the Universe are so far away, almost everything of what we know about them has to do with light. Light is vital for astronomers.

## WHAT'S IT MADE OF?

Light is made up of photons, which can be thought of as little packets of energy. The more photons an object makes, the brighter it is.

Different photons have different amounts of energy, and so will look and behave differently when they interact with matter. When we observe these different behaviours, they tell us a lot about the source of the light!

*The electromagnetic spectrum*

RADIO · MICROWAVE · INFRARED · VISIBLE

**LONGER WAVELENGTH**

WAYS OF SEEING

## LIGHT, PHOTONS AND WHAT WE SEE

Scientists call the range of energy put out by photons the electromagnetic spectrum.

Our eyes can only see a tiny section of this spectrum, which we call optical or visible light. Put simply, every colour you can see is on this part of the spectrum.

All the rest of the photons on the electromagnetic spectrum are invisible to the naked eye.

## INVISIBLE LIGHT?

Why do astronomers care about light our eyes can't see? Because different astronomical events in space put out that kind of light (and may not put out any optical light at all). If we want to understand everything that is happening in our Universe, we can't rely just on our eyes.

So, we build all sorts of instruments to capture light we can't see ourselves and convert it into pictures we can see.

It may seem strange, but in the following pages we'll show you lots of images that we could never see with our own eyes.

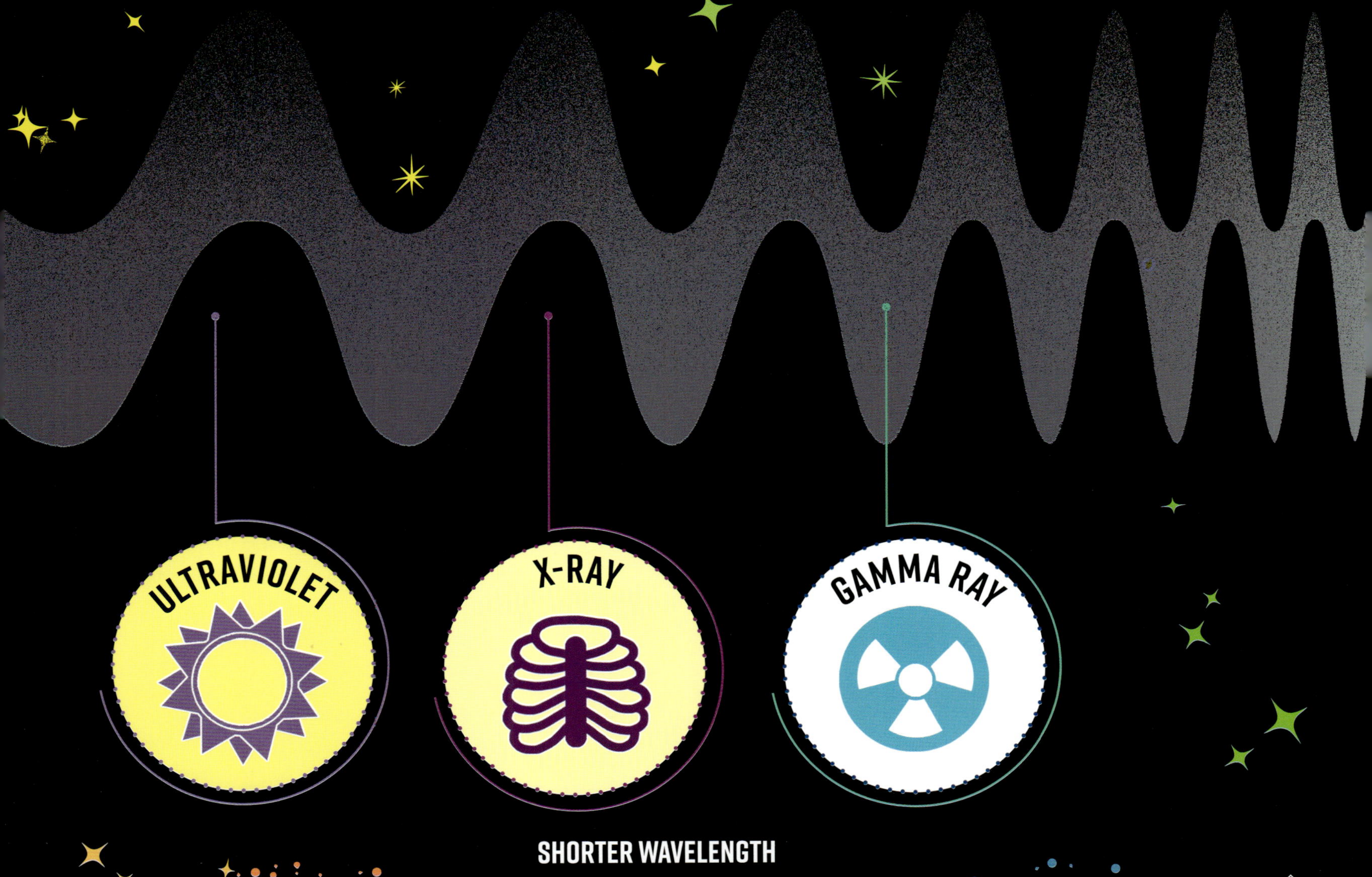

**ULTRAVIOLET**

**X-RAY**

**GAMMA RAY**

**SHORTER WAVELENGTH**

# HUBBLE AND WEBB: TWO UNIQUE VIEWS

———✷———

Earth's atmosphere – the layers of gas that surround our planet – distorts the light passing through it (and even blocks some parts of the electromagnetic spectrum). So telescopes on Earth can't give us the full picture of what's going on in space. One solution: build telescopes that can be sent into space, where the view is clear!

This image was taken with Hubble in 2014. Here, we can see lots of pinkish gases, and bright clusters of stars. These stars light up and shape the rest of the nebula with their intense radiation.

## OLDER AND NEWER

Hubble was launched in 1990, and has produced a huge number of images, expanding our understanding of the Universe with each new set of data it has revealed to us on Earth.

Webb was launched in 2021. Being a bigger and more advanced telescope, it has been able to see fainter objects in more detail than ever before.

This image was taken with Webb in 2022. These shapes may look like mountains, but they are actually vast plumes of gas being carved away by ultraviolet light emitted by newly formed stars.

*A nebula is a cloud-like area where stars are formed in deep space. The Carina Nebula is best seen from Earth's southern hemisphere.*

## NOT JUST A REPLACEMENT

Both telescopes can see some of the visible light that human eyes are capable of seeing, but Hubble also has the ability to see ultraviolet light, while Webb focuses on infrared light. Both perspectives are useful to observe our Universe in ways our own eyes never could.

## TWO TELESCOPES ARE BETTER THAN ONE

Astronomers can use images from both telescopes at once to combine their strengths. These two images are of the same nebula, known as the Carina Nebula. While the Hubble image shows the clouds of the nebula itself in great detail, Webb is capable of peering through those clouds to see the stars forming inside.

# IMPROVING WITH TIME: PILLARS OF CREATION

Hubble may have taken all of these images, but each is very different! Many factors – from updated telescope parts, to the wavelength of light in use – can have a big impact on what we can see in an image, and therefore what we can learn.

On this page are two images of Pillars of Creation: left (in the box) was taken in 1995 and right in 2015.

The increased clarity in the image on the right is thanks to an updated camera on Hubble, allowing for crisp views of different elements that make up the nebula. Astronauts actually upgraded the telescope in space, enabling astronomers back on Earth to take better pictures!

The pillars are five light years tall and are found 7,000 light years away from Earth ...

... but they make up only a small part – less than a tenth – of the Eagle Nebula as a whole.

## SQUARE EYES

Some images of deep space objects seem to have square shapes around the edge. This is because the images aren't just one, but many photos stitched together into a 'mosaic', allowing us to see the bigger picture as well as the detail in each.

Comparing images of the same object taken at different times doesn't just demonstrate how technology has progressed, it also shows how the object itself has changed over time.

WAYS OF SEEING

*This is an infrared light view of Pillars of Creation by Hubble, also taken in 2015, which allows us to uncover a sea of baby stars that would otherwise be hidden within the dusty pillars.*

## A TELESCOPE IN SPACE

Hubble, which is as long as a bus, orbits Earth at a distance of about 515 km. Out in space, views from Hubble aren't obstructed by the Earth's atmosphere. Our atmosphere, which contains moving air, dust, and bad weather, makes our view of space a bit grainy.

## STELLAR CREATION

As you might guess from the name, Pillars of Creation is a place where stars are born. These 'stellar nurseries' contain lots of gas and dust. Regions within these dust clouds start to clump together, and when these clumps get massive enough their own gravity becomes strong enough to form stars!

At the heart of the Orion Nebula is the Trapezium Cluster, a cluster of young, hot stars. It was given this name because, if you draw lines connecting the four brightest stars in the cluster, it makes the shape of a trapezium!

# DIFFERENT INSTRUMENTS

Can you spot the difference between these two images of the Orion Nebula? From Earth, we're able to see this region of star formation with the naked eye, but the Near-Infrared Camera (NIRCam) on board Webb has taken a much closer look. NIRCam captures images using different wavelengths of infrared light, and as a result we can pick out different features of the nebula.

## COUNTING STARS (SHORTER WAVELENGTHS)

The Orion Nebula is home to thousands of young stars. Stars of all sizes are formed here, from stars that can be as small as Jupiter (called red dwarfs), to stars forty times more massive than the Sun! In shorter infrared wavelengths, these stars are bright and easy to spot. The Orion Nebula sits in the middle of the 'sword' hanging from the 'belt' in the Orion constellation, also known as The Hunter, which is visible from almost anywhere in the world, depending on the season.

WAYS OF SEEING

## HOT HYDROGEN! (LONGER WAVELENGTHS)

While the stars in this image appear dimmer, the use of longer wavelengths reveals more detail in the nebula's gas and dust. Towards the centre of the Orion Nebula, there is extremely hot hydrogen gas. Temperatures in this region reach about 10,000°C! Further out, the gas and dust are cooler, seen above in greens and browns.

*The Orion Nebula, captured by Webb using two different wavelengths of infrared light. The nebula is about 1,500 light years from Earth!*

*In here is SOri62! It's one of many free-floating planets found in this nebula. That means it's not actually going around a star – just hanging out alone in this busy nebula.*

# ZOOMING IN: THE HORSEHEAD NEBULA

✱

These are four different views of a stunning swirl in the sky called the Horsehead Nebula. Can you figure out how it got its name? It is a deep-space area of star formation over 1,000 light years from Earth. The colourful clouds you can see are mainly made of hydrogen gas.

## HIDDEN PLANETS

In this wide view, we can see the most star-forming regions in all the images, and astronomers have even spotted some hidden planets, which formed alongside the stars. One is a planet called SOri62. It's ten times more massive than Jupiter and has a temperature of 1,200°C!

*The Horsehead Nebula captured by the European Space Agency's Euclid telescope.*

WAYS OF SEEING

## WHERE ARE WE LOOKING?

If you look at the constellation of Orion in the night sky, you'll see three stars in a nice, neat line making up Orion's belt. The star on the left-hand side of the belt is called Alnitak. With your eyes, you'll see nothing below this star. With a telescope, you could see this huge, cloudy nebula. In the large Euclid image opposite we're seeing just a small fraction of that cloud. In the Hubble image, left, it's a smaller section still!

*Alnitak*

The Horsehead Nebula captured by Hubble.

The Horsehead Nebula captured by Webb.

## HEAD, UP-CLOSE

These images, taken by Webb, are zoomed right in on the 'head' portion of the nebula and show more detail of these beautiful clouds. Astronomers can use these close-ups to study the structures and shapes of these wispy clouds more easily.

# ZOOMING IN: ANDROMEDA GALAXY

On a clear night, we can see our galaxy neighbour with the naked eye: the Andromeda Galaxy. With the fantastic perspective of Hubble, astronomers have captured so much visual information about it just in this one photo.

Towards the galactic centre, things are brighter and denser.

## THE BEST TOOL FOR THE JOB

No telescope can do everything, so astronomers think carefully about the best instrument for the job we want to do. Sometimes we want to see everything in one particular patch of the sky. Or we might want to capture a full picture of one particular object. At other times our goal is to get right up close to a single feature within a larger object.

## WHAT CAN WE SEE OVERALL?

These pictures show selections from part of the Andromeda Galaxy, as seen by Hubble. Hubble captured the light of more than a hundred million of Andromeda's stars (in total, the galaxy may have around a trillion!).

This amazing image also allows us to see star clusters embedded in the galactic structure.

Towards the edge of the galaxy, you can see delicate dust lanes.

The stars aren't in completely random locations, but there's also no strict structure. It's a very complicated picture!

Andromeda is a spiral galaxy. In this extremely high resolution image, taken by Hubble, you can see some of the spiral arm structure.

Compare what you can see here to a picture that shows you the whole galaxy at once (see pages 46–47).

# OUR NEAREST STAR

At an average distance of 150 million km away, the Sun is by far the closest star to us on Earth. That means it's not officially a deep-space object. However, its nearness makes it the easiest star to study and it's an excellent star-starting-point.

## OUR SUN'S SIZE

The Sun is the largest object in our solar system, big enough to contain over one million Earths or more than 1,300 Jupiters! It holds around 99.9% of the mass of the whole solar system. The Sun has so much mass and, therefore, so much gravity, that it can hold our whole solar system together and keep everything orbiting it.

*These images were taken by the Solar Dynamics Observatory using different parts of the electromagnetic spectrum.*

This image shows the transition zone between two of the Sun's layers: the chromosphere and the corona. Together, these form the Sun's outer atmosphere. The corona is the Sun's outermost layer, where temperatures soar to millions of degrees Celsius, far hotter than the surface below. Just beneath the corona lies the chromosphere: a layer of glowing gases that connects the solar surface to the solar atmosphere.

These loops are called solar prominences or filaments. These are places where the Sun's plasma extends outwards in loop shapes.

This is a solar flare, a bright outburst of radiation from the Sun. Solar flares become more and less common over an 11-year solar cycle.

*This image is far into the ultraviolet part of the spectrum, called extreme ultraviolet.*

**STARS AND NEBULAE**

## OUR SUN'S STRUCTURE

Although it looks similar to fire or lava, the Sun is a ball of very hot gases, mostly hydrogen and helium. The immense pressure inside a star squashes these materials together, making new materials and producing energy – enough to power the star, giving off heat and light.

## SEEING IT SAFELY

You should never look at the Sun directly! It produces so much light that it's dangerous for our eyes – and for our telescopes. When we observe the Sun to research it, we use filters that block out most of its light, leaving just a safe amount.

The layer of the Sun that we can see here is called the photosphere. The temperatures range from 3,700-6,200ºC.

These dark patches are called sunspots. They are slightly cooler patches on the Sun's surface.

Sunspots usually come in pairs, with their numbers increasing and decreasing over the same 11-year solar cycle as solar flares.

Sunspots can be anywhere from 16 to 160,000 km in diameter – that's from roughly twice the height of Mount Everest to about 10 times the size of Earth!

*This image uses filtered visible light. The warm orange colour is added to the image by the image processing team.*

# NEXT-DOOR STAR NEIGHBOUR

Beyond our solar system, the closest star to us is in the constellation of Centaurus and is named Proxima Centauri. It is part of a triple star system (three stars that orbit around each other) known as Alpha Centauri. This star is sometimes referred to as 'Alpha Centauri C'.

## CLOSE OR FAR?

Travelling at the speed of light, it would take you a little over four years to reach Proxima Centauri. Because of this, we say that Proxima Centauri is around 4.25 light years away. Light years are a very common unit of distance in astronomy. One light year equals the distance light can travel in one year (around 9.5 trillion km!).

To get to Proxima Centauri with today's space technology, it would take something like 70,000 years!

## CLOSER DOESN'T ALWAYS MEAN BRIGHTER

You might think that the closest star to our solar system would be the brightest in the night sky, but Proxima Centauri is actually too faint to be seen without a telescope. This is because it emits much less light than stars like the Sun, so it appears dimmer to our eyes.

## SOLAR COMPARISON

Stars come in many different sizes. For example, our Sun is roughly seven times wider than Proxima Centauri. The smallest star yet discovered is roughly the size of Jupiter, and the largest is around 3,000 times our Sun's width.

The Sun is a yellow star, but Proxima Centauri is redder. Generally, smaller stars are redder, medium stars are yellow, and larger stars are blue. Proxima Centauri is classed as a red dwarf star.

These are called diffraction spikes (light from the star that has spilled out and across the image). These are caused by the structure of the telescope. We see these in photos, but you wouldn't in real life!

Other bright spots you can see in this image are more distant stars.

*Proxima Centauri, captured by Hubble. Proxima Centauri has at least one – possibly up to three – planets orbiting it.*

# JEWELS IN THE SKY

There are clusters of stars that demonstrate the variety in size, colour and brightness of stars, and the Jewel Box cluster is one of the prettiest examples. It was named by the English astronomer John Herschel, who described the group of stars as looking like 'a superb piece of fancy jewellery'. It is also sometimes referred to as the Kappa Crucis cluster, NGC 4755, or Caldwell 94.

The brightest stars in the cluster form an A-shaped asterism (pattern of stars), with the brightest appearing at the top of the 'A'.

## OBSERVING IT

You can see the Jewel Box cluster with the naked eye. It can be found in Crux (The Cross) constellation, visible from the southern hemisphere, where it looks like a small hazy object. Through binoculars or a telescope, you can start to spot individual stars and see some of the different colours.

This is one of the youngest known clusters in space, with the stars thought to be about 14 million years old. For context, our Sun is around 4.5 billion years old!

## OPEN STAR CLUSTER

The Jewel Box is what we call an open cluster. All the stars are loosely bound to one another through gravity, meaning that they are all orbiting the same point at their shared centre, and they travel around the galaxy in this one group. The stars would have all formed at roughly the same time, in their shared stellar nursery.

The stars in this cluster are around 6,500 light years away from Earth.

This image of the Jewel Box cluster was captured by the European Southern Observatory's La Silla Observatory in Chile.

# STARS FORMING ON A GRAND SCALE

---※---

Stars are not eternal. They have beginnings and ends, and they all change over time in a process known as stellar evolution. To find where stars form, we head back over to a nebula.

## STAR FACTORIES ON THE OUTSKIRTS

This is NGC 602, an open star cluster found within a nebula called N90. We've met a stellar nursery before (see pages 10–17) and an open cluster (see pages 24–25), but this super-crisp and colourful image taken by Webb allows us to see another interesting story.

Gas and dust has been driven out of the middle of N90, which has resulted in star formation happening in the outer ridges of the nebula, rather than from a dense blob in the centre. The gravity of small clumps of material within the outer ridges pulls in more and more dust and gas to grow bigger and eventually become stars.

Star formation near some hot, bright stars shapes gas and dust into a long column. They are sometimes known as 'elephant's trunks'.

STARS AND NEBULAE

## FAILED STARS

Another key observation we can make here is that NGC 602 contains brown dwarfs. These are objects that are too big to be considered planets but are also too small to be considered stars, which is why they're often nicknamed 'failed stars'.

NGC 602 sits outside our own galaxy – the Milky Way (see pages 44–45) – in the Small Magellanic Cloud. This makes it the first place outside our galaxy where brown dwarfs have ever been found, thanks to our increasingly powerful telescopes. As time goes by, we expect to find brown dwarfs in even more distant galaxies!

This image also shows many distant galaxies that seem to dot the sky around NGC 602. In fact, they are much further away from us than NGC 602 is, and are totally unrelated to it.

*Open star cluster NGC 602 captured by Webb.*

*Rho Ophiuchi captured by Webb.*

# THE LOCAL NURSERY

At 390 light years away from Earth, Rho Ophiuchi is the nearest region of star formation to our planet. It is found in the constellation of Ophiuchus, but don't try to spot it with the naked eye – it's impossible to see with visible light. Webb, however, was able to capture this impressive view using infrared light.

## WHAT ARE WE SEEING?

There are about 50 stars in this image, most of which are similar in mass to the Sun. These stars shape the nebula around them, creating this beautiful flower-like structure.

The large red jets we can see come from streams of hydrogen emitted from the poles of young stars.

This is S1, one of the few stars in this region that is more massive than the Sun. It emits powerful ultraviolet radiation, which has sculpted the shape of the yellow dusty region around it.

Buried in the thick clouds of the darker regions, there may be even more stars forming. But the dark regions are hidden from view.

**STARS AND NEBULAE**

# THAT'S A LOT: INSIDE A GLOBULAR CLUSTER

This is a group of stars called Messier 15 (M15). It's what we call a globular cluster. It is a collection of over 100,000 stars held together tightly by their shared gravity. It can be found just beyond the 'nose' in the constellation Pegasus, The Flying Horse, which is best seen from the northern hemisphere.

## OLDER THAN YOU'D THINK

Globular clusters are some of the oldest objects in the Universe, with most of the stars within them forming a very long time ago. M15 is one of the oldest globular clusters ever discovered – it is estimated to be around 12 billion years old!

## BRIGHTER DEEP DOWN

The deeper you travel into a globular cluster, the more tightly packed the stars get. M15 has experienced a 'core collapse', making it really crowded towards the middle and causing some stars to collide.

## HIDDEN BEAST

If we were to fly all the way into the centre of this globular cluster, we would find a rare type of black hole (see pages 36–37 for more). It weighs the same as 4,000 Suns, making it bigger than an ordinary black hole, but smaller than a supermassive black hole. Scientists still don't fully understand how it formed here!

There aren't usually any new stars forming in these clusters, all the stars you can see in them are very old.

*Globular cluster, M15, released by Hubble on 14 November 2013.*

# IT'S LOOKING RIGHT AT ME!

The Cat's Eye Nebula was discovered by William Herschel in 1786, and humans have been studying it ever since. It is an object known as a planetary nebula and shows us one possible end of a star's life cycle.

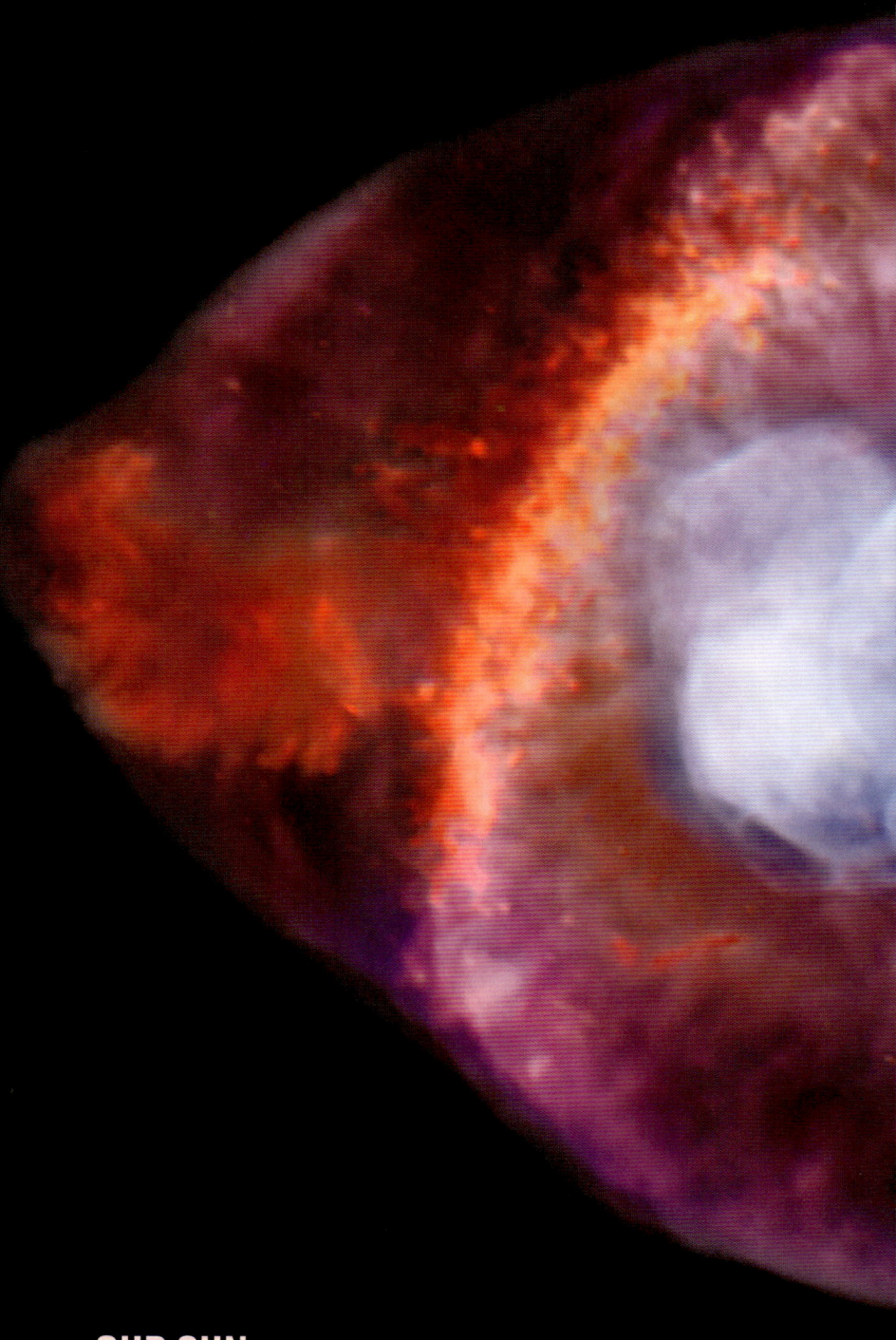

## STAR GLOW

The Cat's Eye Nebula is a dead red giant star. Towards the end of their lives, these stars push off their outer layers and their cores collapse under the intense pull of gravity. This very hot core produces radiation, which causes the gas around it to glow.

In other words, the star makes a wispy shell of gas, then lights it up! The different gases in a nebula emit different colours of light. By looking carefully at a nebula through powerful telescopes, astronomers can see what it is made of.

## WHAT IS A PLANETARY NEBULA?

Early astronomers called these objects planetary nebulae because, using the telescopes available at the time, they looked fuzzy (or 'nebulous'). Many were roughly circular, so they thought they looked like planets (they're not!). Unfortunately, this caught on, and now we're stuck with a name that doesn't really make sense ...

## OUR SUN

Astronomers believe that the Sun will eventually produce a planetary nebula after it becomes a red giant and the core collapses to become a white dwarf. No two nebulae look exactly the same, so we don't know if ours will be quite as lovely as the Cat's Eye Nebula.

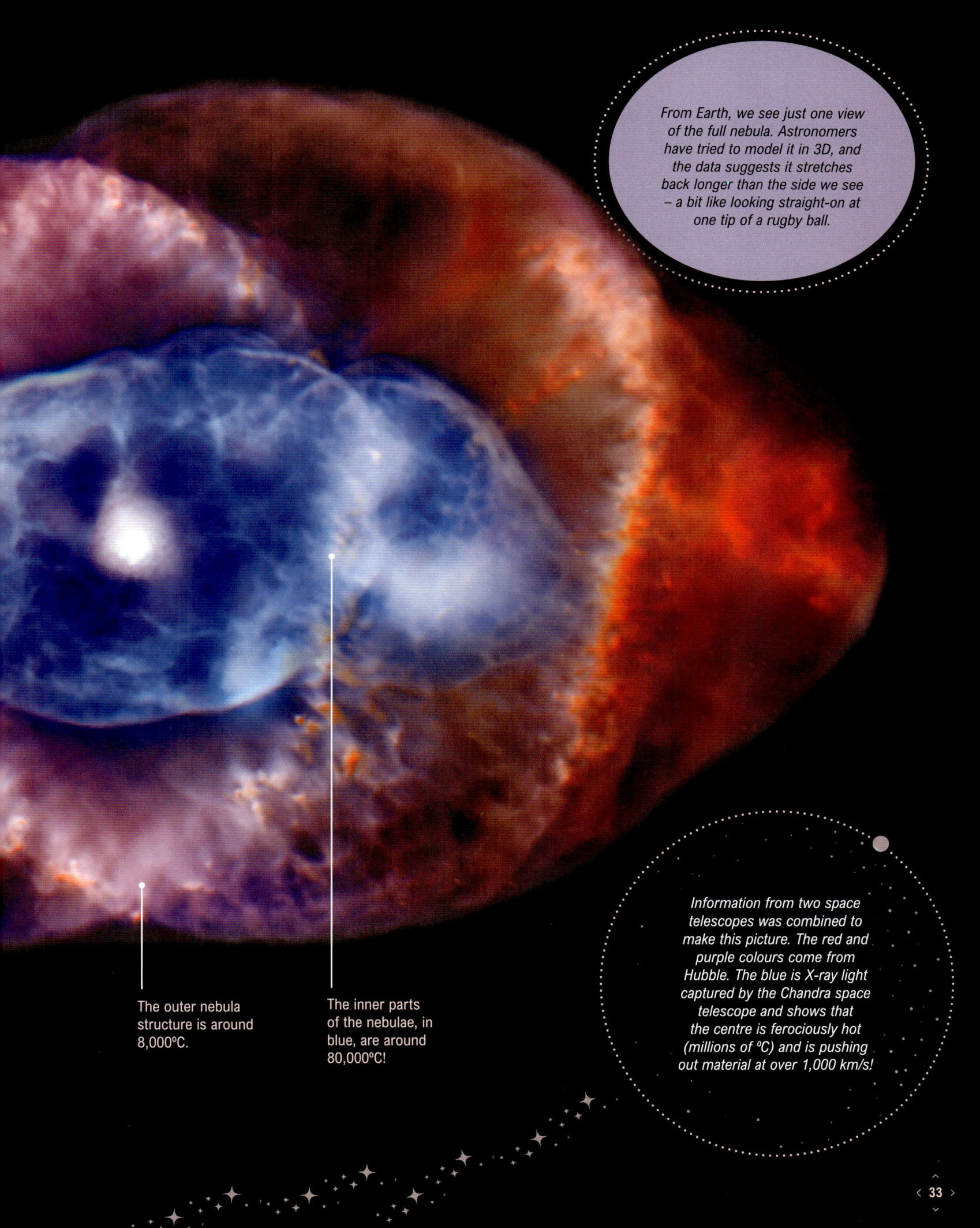

From Earth, we see just one view of the full nebula. Astronomers have tried to model it in 3D, and the data suggests it stretches back longer than the side we see – a bit like looking straight-on at one tip of a rugby ball.

The outer nebula structure is around 8,000ºC.

The inner parts of the nebulae, in blue, are around 80,000ºC!

Information from two space telescopes was combined to make this picture. The red and purple colours come from Hubble. The blue is X-ray light captured by the Chandra space telescope and shows that the centre is ferociously hot (millions of ºC) and is pushing out material at over 1,000 km/s!

Here's the white dwarf in each image.

# SPOT THE DIFFERENCE

Here are two images of the same planetary nebula. This is another dying star, like the Cat's Eye Nebula we've already seen. This one is called the Southern Ring Nebula. It's around 2,000 light years away from us and it used to be a star similar to the Sun, before it started to run out of fuel and shed its outer layers.

## WHY TWO?

Both of these images were taken at the same time in July 2022 by Webb. They both use infrared light rather than light our eyes can see, but they were captured using different instruments on the telescope. The two instruments use slightly different parts of the infrared spectrum. Astronomers choose to do this so they can see different features. What differences can you spot?

STARS AND NEBULAE

*Two images of the Southern Ring Nebula taken by Webb.*

## STARS TO SPOT

The white dwarf star, which is the core of the original star now dying and spreading out across space, is visible in both of these images, though it looks much smaller on page 34.

There's also a second star you can see in the centre of both images. This star and its white dwarf companion create a binary system (two stars orbiting each other). In this case, the second star hasn't yet shed its outer layers, so it's the bigger and brighter star in both images.

## DUST

One difference between these two images is how much dust is visible. The photo on the right-hand side focuses on the dust in the planetary nebula. The dwarf star appears bigger in this photo because the dust around it is emphasised. Additionally, the other stars around the nebula seem dimmer in comparison to the photo on the left-hand side.

# DON'T FALL IN!

This is the first picture taken of a black hole – an object notoriously difficult to photograph! Known as M87*, it is at the centre of a galaxy 50 million light years away from Earth.

*The supermassive black hole M87*, is at the centre of galaxy M87, and was captured here by the Event Horizon Telescope in 2019.*

## DRAMATICALLY DEAD STAR

When stars that are at least eight times heavier than our Sun die, they have a much more chaotic end than small stars (which end up as planetary nebulae, like the Cat's Eye Nebula on pages 34–35).

Massive stars die in a huge explosion known as a supernova. As they age, they build up heavy material that they can't use as fuel in their cores, such as iron.

Eventually, when the gravity of the elements in their core is too strong and the stars can no longer support their own weight, the centre of the star collapses, causing the rest of the star to explode!

The core of the star that has collapsed, if it is massive enough, turns into a black hole.

## EXTREME GRAVITY

Black holes are extremely dense; they have more matter than our Sun, all shoved into a tiny volume. This means they have super-strong gravity! A black hole's gravity is so strong that not even light can escape – this is where they got their name.

If you were to get too close to a black hole you would get spaghettified, meaning the gravity is so strong it would stretch you into a piece of spaghetti!

## SUPERMASSIVE!

Some black holes are much bigger than even the largest stars, which means they have grown over time, likely by gobbling up gas, dust and even other whole stars.

M87* is over 6 million times the mass of our Sun, which means it must have ripped apart and eaten the equivalent of millions of stars!

**STARS AND NEBULAE**

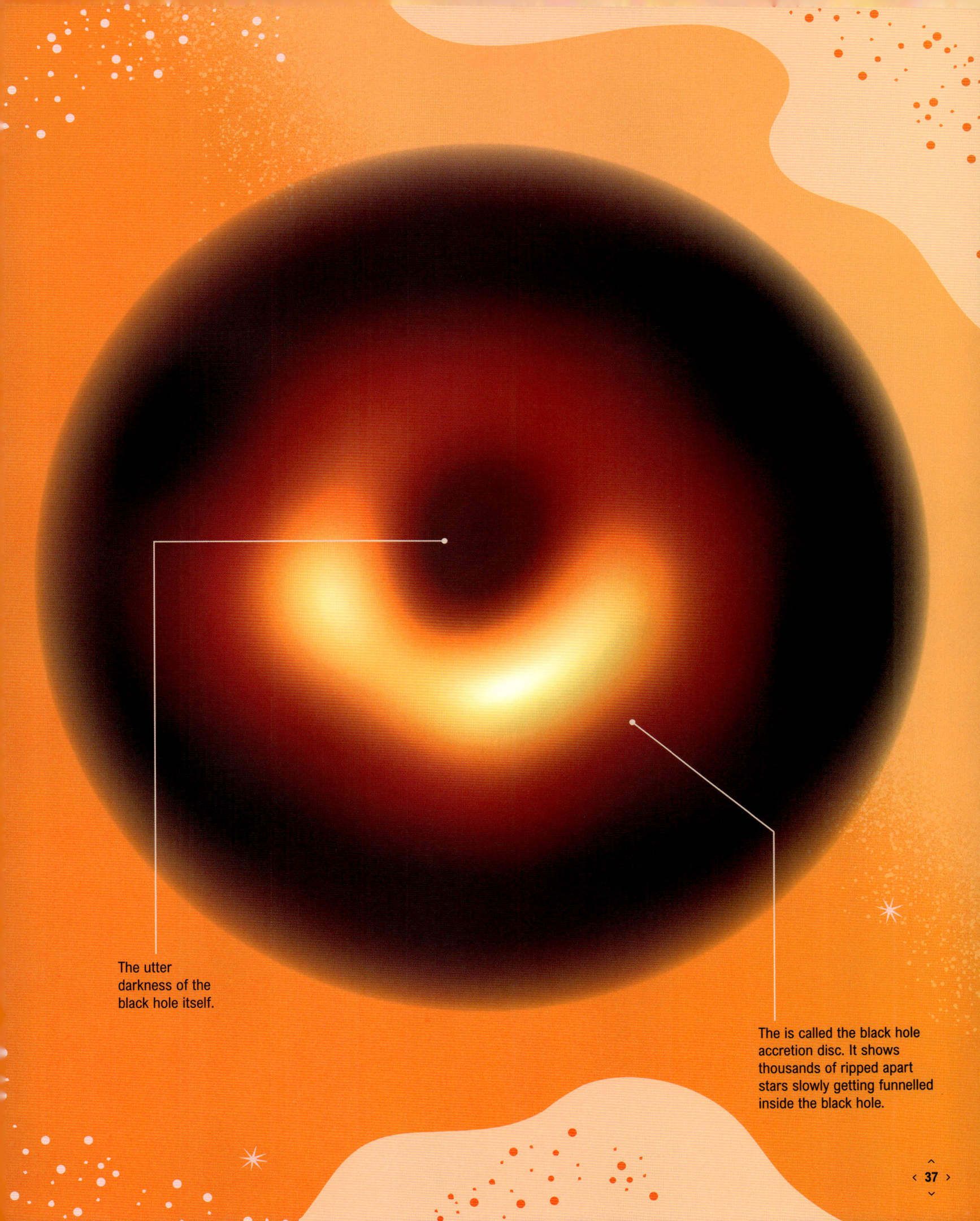

The utter darkness of the black hole itself.

The is called the black hole accretion disc. It shows thousands of ripped apart stars slowly getting funnelled inside the black hole.

# IT'S HISTORY!

The Crab Nebula is a supernova's leftovers (called a remnant). Amazingly, enough people all over the world wrote about seeing the explosion in the sky at the time that we can be almost certain the light from the supernova became visible on Earth in 1054 CE. Because we know how old it is, we can calculate the speed at which certain processes occurred to form the nebula we see from Earth today.

*A composite of data collected from Hubble, and infrared data from Webb.*

## DISCOVERING NEBULAE

The Crab Nebula is very roughly spherical, but it's quite clumpy in places and a bit less dense in others. That means, in the image here, you can see material that is hurtling towards us, but you can also see *through* parts of the nebula to the material travelling away from us.

## INSIDE THE CAGE OF DUST

Strands of dust created by the supernova explosion create a complicated cage shape. Some other structures inside the nebula are shaped by the cage, but other structures are caused more by the radiation of the exploded star.

## SPEEDY PIECES

The star has become a rapidly spinning object called a pulsar, rotating 360° every 33 milliseconds (much less than the blink of an eye!). The pulsar is slowing down very gradually. It currently 'pulses' about 30 times a second. If the slowing continues at this rate, in about 100 years it will be down to 29 times a second.

STARS AND NEBULAE

You can't see the pulsar itself here, but you can see radiation from very fast-moving charged particles (seen in blue) shaped by the pulsar's powerful magnetic field as it spins.

The dust is coloured pink, and you can see it is denser in the thread-like structures.

Green shows sulphur.

# WHERE DOES A ZOMBIE STAR COME FROM?

Kaboom! This is a star-burst-style supernova remnant, discovered in 2013 but tied to an explosion observed by ancient astronomers in 1183 CE!

The left-behind zombie star that survived the supernova explosion.

This is a composite image of Pa 30, the remnant of supernova 1183, combining observations from multiple space and ground-based telescopes.

## A DIFFERENT TYPE OF SUPERNOVA

Many supernovas, like the one that created the Crab Nebula (see pages 38–39) were caused by a really big star exploding. But there's another way to make stars explode – even small ones like our Sun!

When a white dwarf is in a binary pair, similar to the pair in the middle of the Southern Ring Nebula (see pages 34–35), the gravity of the white dwarf will attract material from the partner star. This is called accreting the material. The white dwarf can accrete enough material to the point that it becomes so massive that it explodes in a supernova.

## ZOMBIE STAR LEFTOVERS

Typically, a white dwarf supernova is so powerful that the star gets completely destroyed, leaving nothing behind! In the case of this supernova, looking into the centre reveals there actually is a star that survived the explosion – known as a zombie star.

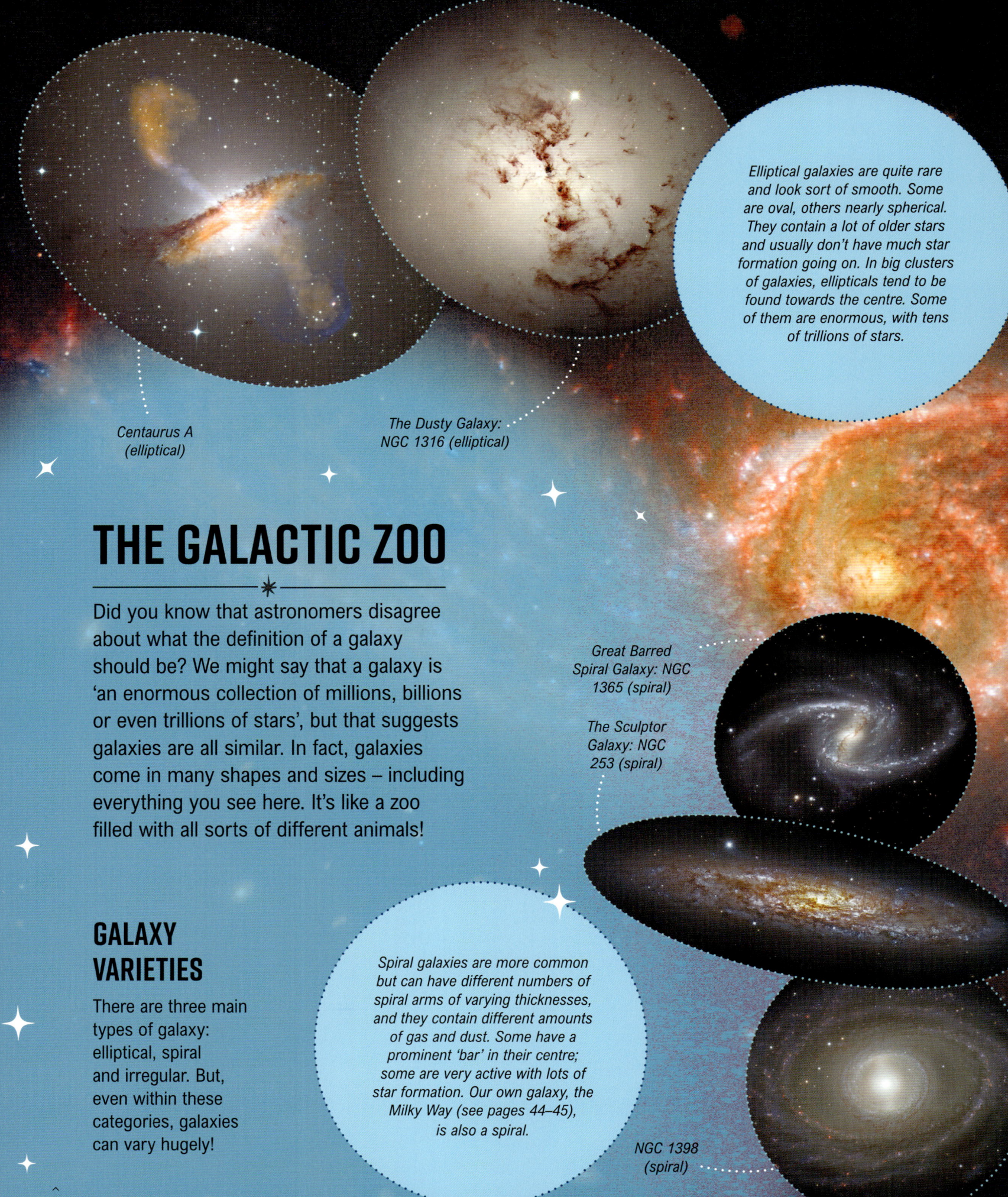

*Centaurus A (elliptical)*

*The Dusty Galaxy: NGC 1316 (elliptical)*

Elliptical galaxies are quite rare and look sort of smooth. Some are oval, others nearly spherical. They contain a lot of older stars and usually don't have much star formation going on. In big clusters of galaxies, ellipticals tend to be found towards the centre. Some of them are enormous, with tens of trillions of stars.

# THE GALACTIC ZOO

Did you know that astronomers disagree about what the definition of a galaxy should be? We might say that a galaxy is 'an enormous collection of millions, billions or even trillions of stars', but that suggests galaxies are all similar. In fact, galaxies come in many shapes and sizes – including everything you see here. It's like a zoo filled with all sorts of different animals!

*Great Barred Spiral Galaxy: NGC 1365 (spiral)*

*The Sculptor Galaxy: NGC 253 (spiral)*

## GALAXY VARIETIES

There are three main types of galaxy: elliptical, spiral and irregular. But, even within these categories, galaxies can vary hugely!

Spiral galaxies are more common but can have different numbers of spiral arms of varying thicknesses, and they contain different amounts of gas and dust. Some have a prominent 'bar' in their centre; some are very active with lots of star formation. Our own galaxy, the Milky Way (see pages 44–45), is also a spiral.

*NGC 1398 (spiral)*

GALAXIES

Irregular galaxies are those without a regular structure like the others. They can have all sorts of shapes and may include spiral structures ... but not always.

The Spider Galaxy: UGC 5829 (irregular)

Dwarf Galaxy UGC 8091 (irregular)

Spiral galaxy IC 2163 (left) passing behind spiral galaxy NGC 2207 (right) using information from Webb and Hubble.

# UNDERSTANDING GALAXIES

So, can we say anything about galaxies for certain? Because they are so big, so far away, and they change so slowly, astronomers only really get one view of a galaxy. But, by comparing the many billions of galaxies we can see, we can work out how they tend to change and the different things that shape them.

*The Milky Way panorama, from the GigaGalaxy Zoom project by European Southern Observatory (ESO), showing the full view of the Milky Way from Earth.*

*Centre of our Milky Way Galaxy*

# THE MILKY WAY

Our home in space, the Milky Way Galaxy, is a vast area of gas, dust and stars. Although we've never travelled outside our galaxy to view it from afar, we think it looks like neighbouring Andromeda, with beautiful spiral arms and a bulky centre. But what can we see from our perspective inside the galaxy? A lot!

## IT'S ALL ABOUT PERSPECTIVE!

Since the Sun (and you and I!) live in one of the Milky Way's arms, we see the galaxy edge-on as a band of light, sprinkled with dark patches, in the sky.

*Astronomers think there are as many as 400 billion stars in our galaxy.*

## LIGHT AND DARK

The light we see comes from billions of stars, including many bright, young stars. The dark patches are interstellar dust that sits between us and the galaxy's centre.

Astronomers use telescopes capable of piercing through the dust to look at stars in the Milky Way and have spotted evidence of a supermassive black hole called Sagittarius A*, which sits at the heart of our galaxy.

## HOW BIG IS THE MILKY WAY?

Astronomers think our Milky Way is more than 100,000 light years across, which means it would take light over 100,000 years to travel from one edge to the other. But it is only about 1,000 light years thick on average, so the Milky Way probably looks a bit like a fried egg!

This picture also shows us M110, a dwarf satellite galaxy, which is orbiting Andromeda. It is much smaller than Andromeda, containing a relatively measly 10 billion stars.

# OUR GALACTIC NEIGHBOUR

Our nearest neighbouring galaxy lies a whopping 2.5 million light years away from us. We saw an up-close view of the Andromeda Galaxy on page 18–19, but here we zoom out to get a much wider picture of it, a galaxy that contains an estimated one trillion stars! By studying it we can begin to learn more about our own Milky Way and what the future may hold for both galaxies.

## A CITY OF STARS

The Andromeda Galaxy has more than twice as many stars as the Milky Way. The stars can be found winding along Andromeda's spiral arms of dust and gas, the raw material from which the stars formed.

## COLLISION INBOUND

Did you know that the Andromeda galaxy is coming towards us right now? It's true! It gets about 100 km closer to us every second. We are on a direct collision course with Andromeda, but luckily, because of how far away it is, it won't hit us for another 4.5 billion years or so.

*Wide-field view of the Andromeda Galaxy captured by Hubble.*

*The Pinwheel Galaxy captured by Hubble.*

# GALACTIC LOOKALIKE

✳

This image shows the Pinwheel Galaxy, a stunning spiral galaxy containing around one trillion stars. It is 25 million light years away from Earth, and observers in the northern hemisphere see it inside the constellation of Ursa Major (also known as The Great Bear). It is similar to the Milky Way and the Andromeda Galaxy in some ways, but very different in other ways.

## A GRAND DESIGN

Named for its distinctive pinwheel shape, the Pinwheel Galaxy is known as a 'grand design spiral'. This means that it has eye-catching and well-defined spiral arms of dust and gas that swirl outwards from its centre.

## A GALACTIC FACE-OFF

How much we can learn about a galaxy often depends on the angle of it we see from Earth. Our view is something that we can't change. Fortunately for us, we see the Pinwheel Galaxy almost exactly face-on (instead of edge-on), making it a lot easier to study and investigate.

## BABY STARS GALORE

As if one trillion stars wasn't enough, the Pinwheel Galaxy is also packed with over 3,000 enormous star-forming regions, which are all producing brand-new stars.

This might be partly because of close encounters with other galaxies whose gravity has disrupted the distribution of gas and dust in the Pinwheel Galaxy. This creates or fuels stellar nurseries, which in turn triggers a huge surge in star formation. The fact that the Pinwheel Galaxy isn't symmetrical is evidence for these close encounters, but it isn't entirely clear how often they have occurred, or exactly when.

It is believed that a supermassive black hole may lie at the centre of this galaxy, but it has not yet been officially observed or confirmed to exist.

# GALACTIC CRASH

The Antennae Galaxies are in the process of colliding. Originally, they were two entirely separate spiral galaxies, but around a billion years ago they started to merge. This crash process will continue for millions more years until the two galaxies have fully combined into one larger, elliptical-shaped galaxy. Astronomers have observed many galaxies that have collided in the past, or will in the future, but the Antennae Galaxies are colliding right now!

## SWIRLING STAR FORMATION

This image shows clouds of gas from both galaxies swirling together in pink and red.

Clouds of blue show places where new stars are being formed. When galaxies merge like this, it triggers a lot of new stars to form and changes the shape of the galaxies – stars are strewn out across space. You can see the streams of stars stretching out in the photo.

On average, stars are so far apart that the chance of any two stars directly hitting each other when the galaxies collide is extremely small. The galaxies don't get smashed up as two solid objects might; they disrupt each other because of gravity. Eventually, where there were two separate galaxies, a large, newly shaped single galaxy will remain.

*The Antennae Galaxies, also called NGC 4038 and NGC 4039, imaged here by Hubble, are about 62 million light years from Earth.*

*When the Milky Way and Andromeda galaxies merge billions of years from now, astronomers think the new combined galaxy will need a new name. What do you think it should be called?*

Here's one of the many areas with new stars forming.

# CLUSTERS OF CLUSTERS

---✱---

Just as stars bunch up into clusters within galaxies, many galaxies are found in clusters as well. These three galaxies, known as the Leo Triplet, are a great example.

## A COSMIC TAPE MEASURE

When we look at objects in space, it is really difficult to tell how far away they are. Things that seem close together in the sky may be very far apart, one much closer to us than the other. Astronomers use a lot of different ways of measuring distances to build out an imaginary tape measure long enough to stretch across the cosmos. For the Leo Triplet, astronomers found that the galaxies were all about 35 million light years from Earth and close enough together to be their own cluster.

*The Leo Triplet is a group of galaxies found just under the constellation of Leo, The Lion, which is visible in the northern hemisphere skies.*

While all three galaxies are spiral galaxies, we are seeing them from different angles. This one is seen almost perfectly edge-on.

## TOGETHER FOREVER?

These three galaxies remain in a tight group due to their gravity constantly pulling on each other. A bit like the planets orbiting the Sun, they orbit each other and, unless something dramatically changes, they will continue to behave this way.

## BUMPS AND SCRAPES

Being so close together, it's not surprising that every now and then, these galaxies will bash into each other. At least two of them show signs of having passed very close together, their gravity distorting each other, slightly bending the galaxy on the top right (NGC 3628) and pulling apart the spiral arms of the galaxy in the top left (NGC 3627).

The light from more distant galaxies has taken longer to reach us. We can see galaxies that are more than 12 billion years old.

## HOW MANY?

There are almost 10,000 galaxies in this image, each a collection of millions, billions, or even trillions of stars. What's even more amazing is that this picture captures only a tiny fraction of the number of galaxies in our night sky.

How did we do it? To capture all these galaxies, Hubble focused on a very small patch of sky and collected light from the galaxies for 11.3 days in total to produce this image.

## WHAT FOR?

This type of photo is called an 'ultra deep field' image because it's looking at things incredibly far away from Earth, in other words: deep into space. Before astronomers were able to take this type of photo, we had never seen most of these galaxies, and we didn't realise how many there would be.

We can use photos like this to work out what the Universe was like billions of years ago, as some of the galaxies shown are billions of years old. We can also use it to estimate the total number of galaxies in the Universe, through some clever multiplication – perhaps as many as 2 trillion!

*Ultra Deep Field image taken by Hubble.*

Different varieties of galaxies are also visible. What shapes can you see? (You can review the three galaxy types on pages 42–43.)

There are a few individual stars from the Milky Way in this image – you can spot them as they have diffraction spikes coming from them, like this one (see pages 22–23).

Everything else you can see in this image is an entire galaxy!

55

# MAPPING THE NEIGHBOURHOOD

———✳———

This unique map of our neighbourhood, the Milky Way, was created by the Gaia space observatory. It shows the density of our galaxy (how 'packed together' things are) more accurately than we'd ever seen it previously.

## OBSERVATORY IN SPACE!

The Gaia space observatory observed the skies from out in space near Earth for 10 years, from 2015–25. Its mission was to map the locations of billions of stars in our galaxy – and also their motion!

The faint curved lines are caused by Gaia observing lots of small patches across the sky and stitching them together to make one big image. They do not represent a real pattern in our galaxy.

*The density of the Milky Way – image created by ESA's Gaia space telescope.*

The 'galactic bulge' where the majority of stars in our galaxy live, surrounding a supermassive black hole.

## A DIFFERENT MAP

Some stars are much bigger and brighter than others, so when we look at normal images, they can outshine stars that are less bright or further away. But in this image, every star is shown with the same brightness so we can see the true density of our galaxy.

## RETIREMENT

In 2025, Gaia went into retirement. It was moved from its position close to Earth, into an orbit around the Sun far out of the way of other hard-working space-based observatories.

These two bright patches are the Large and Small Magellanic Clouds, dwarf galaxies that orbit our Milky Way.

*A view of the sky from Earth, showing only the 2MASS galaxies. You can see how they are all around us (and a gap where the Milky Way got in the way of the survey's view!).*

# WHAT ABOUT FURTHER OUT?

In 1997, scientists set out to look at the entire sky using only infrared radiation. The project was called the Two Micron All-Sky Survey (2MASS), and it was a huge success! This method detected more than 1.5 million galaxies, allowing us to look more than a billion light years into space, and resulted in these astounding images. Every dot you see is a galaxy.

2MASS collected three types of infrared wavelength light. This allowed it to see through interstellar dust, which would normally get in the way.

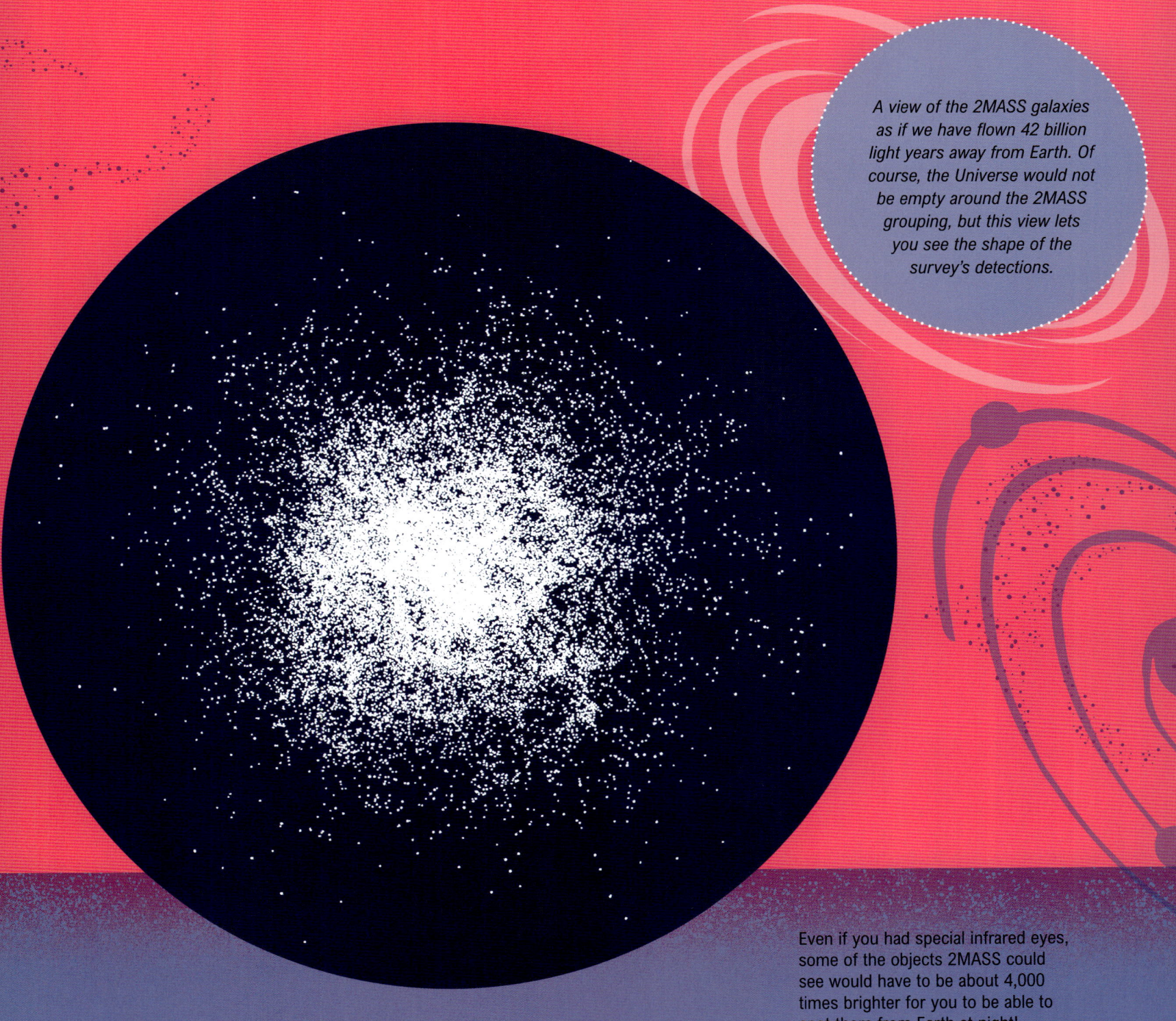

A view of the 2MASS galaxies as if we have flown 42 billion light years away from Earth. Of course, the Universe would not be empty around the 2MASS grouping, but this view lets you see the shape of the survey's detections.

Even if you had special infrared eyes, some of the objects 2MASS could see would have to be about 4,000 times brighter for you to be able to spot them from Earth at night!

## MAP-MAKING ... IN SPACE!

2MASS scanned the sky over a few years using its infrared detectors. This was used to produce a map of the local Universe. We say 'local' because, while the map is impressive in size, it is still very small compared to the size of the entire Universe.

2MASS not only spotted objects and galaxies but figured out their distance from us. This means the full map is actually three-dimensional!

## GALAXY WEBS

One of the most interesting things that you can see from the map is that the Universe is a bit 'webby'. Galaxies cluster together, and on very large scales they line up in thread-like patterns. They aren't physically connected, but they also aren't spaced out equally, nor are they in completely random positions.

This is important information for astronomers because seeing the positions of galaxies today helps us learn about the development of the early Universe.

# HOW FAR CAN WE GO?

───────── ✶ ─────────

When the Universe was very young it was too hot for atoms to form. Light was trapped in a sea of opaque matter, bouncing around constantly. When the Universe was almost half a million years old, it had cooled down enough for atoms to form and the Universe became transparent. Light was finally free to move around. This is the first moment it was possible to 'see' the Universe.

Today, we can still see all the way back to this moment!

The CMBR is almost the same temperature in every direction: -270.45ºC (extremely cold). The slightly hotter (red) and colder (blue) bits shown here are only different by a tiny fraction of a degree. Temperature differences are exaggerated in the picture so we aren't just looking at one colour!

## TOUCHING THE LIMITS

The Universe continued to cool and expand, so those first visible photons became microwaves. (If this hadn't happened, the entire night sky would shine like the Sun!) The microwaves have also expanded in all directions. This layer of microwaves is like a bubble of light that surrounds us. We call it the Cosmic Microwave Background Radiation (CMBR).

## THE END?

We can't see beyond the CMBR, because that would be looking back to a time before those photons could move freely.

This doesn't mean there is an 'end' to the Universe. It means there is a limit to how far back in time we can see using light. Ultimately, viewing the whole Universe is impossible.

The spheres you see below are rotated views of a 3–D map of the CMBR. This was mapped by the Planck space observatory mission.

Tiny differences reveal where matter was more or less dense at this moment. These clumps affected how the Universe developed.

If the Universe was perfectly smooth, it wouldn't have formed the clusters of galaxies we have today in the same way. The whole Universe would look very different.

# GLOSSARY

**Black hole**
A place in space where gravity is so strong that not even light can escape.

**Constellation**
A pattern of stars in the sky named after animals, people, or objects.

**Cosmic dust**
Tiny particles of matter floating in space, often found in nebulae.

**Dark matter**
Invisible stuff that doesn't give off light but has gravity and holds galaxies together.

**Electromagnetic spectrum**
All types of light, including visible light, radio waves, X-rays, and more.

**Filament**
A huge thread-like structure made of gas and dark matter that connects galaxies across the Universe.

**Galaxy**
A huge group of stars, planets, gas and dust held together by gravity. We live in the Milky Way Galaxy.

**Gravity**
The force that pulls objects toward each other. This affects the way objects orbit each other.

**Infrared light**
A type of light we can't see with our eyes but we can feel some of it as heat.

**Light year**
The distance light travels in one year – about 9.5 trillion kilometres!

**Matter**
Physical substances that take up space and have mass.

**Nebula**
A giant cloud of gas and dust in space.

**Pulsar**
A spinning neutron star that sends out regular bursts of radio waves.

**Radiation**
The emission of electromagnetic waves or particles, especially high-energy particles.

**Spectroscope**
An instrument attached to telescopes that splits light into colours to show what stars and planets are made of.

**Stellar nursery**
A nebula that is collapsing in some parts because of gravity, causing the gas and dust to clump together and heat up, and eventually giving birth to new stars and planets.

**Supernova**
An enormous explosion when a star runs out of fuel and blasts apart.

**Telescope**
A tool that helps us see distant objects in space by collecting light.

# QUICK QUIZ

**1. What is the name of the galaxy we live in?**
a) Andromeda
b) Whirlpool
c) Milky Way
d) Sombrero

**2. What does the Hubble Space Telescope mostly use to take pictures of space?**
a) X-rays
b) Radio waves
c) Visible light
d) Sound waves

**3. What kind of telescope is the James Webb Space Telescope?**
a) Radio
b) Infrared
c) Microwave
d) Gamma ray

**4. What is a nebula?**
a) A type of comet
b) A giant space rock
c) A cloud of gas and dust
d) A spaceship

**5. What happens in a supernova?**
a) A planet gets destroyed
b) A star runs out of fuel and explodes
c) Two galaxies crash into each other
d) A telescope sends back pictures

**6. Which type of electromagnetic radiation is just beyond the visible spectrum and can cause sunburn?**
a) Gamma rays
b) Ultraviolet
c) Visible light
d) X-rays

**7. What is a black hole?**
a) A hole in space that sucks up time
b) A place where stars are born
c) A region of space with gravity so strong nothing can escape
d) A big empty bubble

**8. Which telescope has set the record for the most distant object seen to date?**
a) Hubble
b) James Webb
c) Galileo's telescope
d) Chandra

**9. Why do we use different parts of the electromagnetic spectrum to study space?**
a) Because space is noisy
b) Because each type of wave shows different things
c) To map the whole sky using infrared light
d) Because Earth blocks visible light

**10. What was the main goal of the 2MASS survey?**
a) To look for aliens using radio signals
b) To photograph planets in our solar system
c) To conduct an infrared survey across the whole sky
d) To study the Sun's magnetic field

# FURTHER INFORMATION

**Books:**

*Wonders of the Moon* (2025)
*Wonders of the Night Sky* (2022)
*The Future of the Universe* (2022)

By Professor Raman Prinja and Jan Bielecki with Royal Observatory Greenwich and Wayland

*The Space Traveller's Guide* series
By Giles Sparrow, Wayland 2025

*Super Tech: Space*
By Clive Gifford, Wayland 2024

**Image archives:**

European Space Agency images:
www.esa.int/ESA_Multimedia/Images

National Aeronautics and Space Administration images:
www.nasa.gov/images

European Southern Observatory images:
www.eso.org/public/images

The home of Hubble/Webb images:
esahubble.org/images

Astronomy Picture of the Day:
apod.nasa.gov/apod/astropix.html
(not only deep space, but there's a huge archive of cool stuff).

**Free, online maps of the night sky, to locate the objects discussed in the book:**

World Wide Telescope:
worldwidetelescope.org

Stellarium:
stellarium-web.org

**We also have lots of fun things here (it says schools and communities, but they're for anyone to enjoy):**

www.rmg.co.uk/schools-communities/schools-resources

**And we put out videos about all sorts of space stuff here:**

www.youtube.com/@RoyalObservatoryGrnwich

# IMAGE AND DATA CREDITS

Cover, p1 Title page and p26 Star formation on a grand scale: ESA/Webb, NASA & CSA, P. Zeidler, E. Sabbi, A. Nota, M. Zamani (ESA/Webb)

P5 Foreword: NASA, ESA, CSA, STScI, Michael Ressler (NASA-JPL), Dave Jones (IAC)

p6 Timeline of space photography: p6 First solar eclipse, First photo of Earth: public domain, p6 First view of the far side of the Moon, first colour image of earth from the Moon: NASA, p7 Ground-based view of stars: NASA, E. Persson (Las Campanas Observatory, Chile)/Observatories of the Carnegie Institution of Washington, p7 First Hubble image: HST, NASA, ESA and STScI, p7 First Webb: Space Telescope Science Institute / NASA, ESA, CSA, STScI, Webb ERO

p10 Hubble and Webb: NASA, ESA, N. Smith (UC Berkeley) and the Hubble Heritage Team (STScI/AURA)

p11 Hubble and Webb: NASA, ESA, CSA, STScI

p12 Improving with time: Pillars of Creation: (bottom left) NASA, ESA/Hubble, STScI, J. Hester and P. Scowen (Arizona State University), (main image) NASA, ESA/Hubble and the Hubble Heritage Team

p13 Improving with time: Pillars of Creation: NASA, ESA/Hubble and the Hubble Heritage Team

pp14–15 Different instruments: NASA, ESA, CSA / Science leads and image processing: M. McCaughrean, S. Pearson

pp16–17 Zooming in: The Horsehead Nebula: (left) ESA/Euclid/ Euclid Consortium/ NASA, image processing by J.-C. Cuillandre (CEA Paris-Saclay), G. Anselmi; (top right) NASA, ESA, and the Hubble Heritage Team (AURA/ STScI); (bottom left and right) NASA, ESA, CSA, K. Misselt

p18 Zooming in: Andromeda Galaxy: NASA, ESA, J. Dalcanton (University of Washington, USA), B. F. Williams (University of Washington, USA), L. C. Johnson (University of Washington, USA), the PHAT team, and R. Gendler

pp20–21 Our nearest star: NASA, SDO/AIA

pp22–23 Next-door star neighbour: NASA, ESA

pp24–25 Jewels in the sky: ESO

pp28–29 The local nursery: NASA, ESA, CSA, STScI, Klaus Pontoppidan (STScI)

pp30–31 That's a lot: Inside a globular cluster: NASA, ESA

pp32–33 It's looking right at me: X-ray: NASA/CXC/SAO, Optical: NASA/STScI

pp34–35 Spot the difference: NASA, ESA, CSA, STScI, and the Webb ERO Production Team

p37 Don't fall in:
EHT Collaboration

pp38–39 It's history: NASA, ESA, CSA, STScI, T. Temim (Princeton University)

pp40–41 Where does a zombie star come from?: G. Ferrand and J. English (U. of Manitoba), NASA/Chandra/WISE, ESA/XMM, MDM/R. Fessen (Dartmouth College), Pan-STARRS

p42 Galactic zoo: (top left) ESO/WFI (Optical), MPIfR/ESO/APEX/A.Weiss et al (Submillimetre), NASA/CXC/CfA/R.Kraft et al (X-ray); (top centre) NASA, ESA, and The Hubble Heritage Team (STScI/AURA); Acknowledgments: P. Goudfrooij (STScI); (bottom right: top, centre and bottom) ESO United Kingdom

p43 Galactic zoo: (top left) ESA/Hubble, NASA Y. Choi (NOIRLab), K. Gilbert (Space Telescope Science Institute), J. Dalcanton (Flatiron Institute and University of Washington); (top centre) ESA/Hubble & NASA, R. Tully, M. Messa, (background pp42–43): NASA, ESA, CSA, STScI

pp44–45 The Milky Way: ESO/VVV Survey/D. Minniti. Acknowledgements: Ignacio Toledo, Martin Kornmesser

pp46–47 Our galactic neighbour: ESA/Hubble & Digitized Sky Survey 2; Acknowledgment: Davide De Martin (ESA/Hubble)

pp48–49 Galactic lookalike: European Space Agency & NASA; Acknowledgements: Project Investigators for the original Hubble data: K.D. Kuntz (GSFC), F. Bresolin (University of Hawaii), J. Trauger (JPL), J. Mould (NOAO), and Y.-H. Chu (University of Illinois, Urbana) Image processing: Davide De Martin (ESA/Hubble) CFHT image: Canada-France-Hawaii Telescope/J.-C. Cuillandre/Coelum NOAO image: George Jacoby, Bruce Bohannan, Mark Hanna/NOAO/AURA/NSF

pp50–51 Galactic crash: Credit: ESA/Hubble, NASA

pp52–53 Clusters of clusters: Credit: ESO, INAF-VST, OmegaCAM; Acknowledgements: OmegaCen, Astro-WISE, Kapteyn I

pp54–55 How many: NASA, ESA, and S. Beckwith (STScI) and the HUDF Team

pp56–57 Mapping the neighbourhood: ESA/Gaia/DPAC; CC BY-SA 3.0 IGO; Acknowledgements: A. Moitinho and M. Barros

pp58–59 What about further out?: 2MASS/UMass/ipaac-Caltech/NASA/NSF

pp60–61 How far can we go?: ESA, NASA/LAMBDA, WMAP, NASA

# INDEX

**A**
Alnitak 17
Alpha Centauri 22
Antennae Galaxies 50–1
Andromeda Galaxy 18–19, 44, 50
asterism 24
astronaut 12
astronomers 34
atoms 60

**B**
Berkowski, Julius 6
binary system 35, 41
black hole 30, 36–7, 49, 57
brown dwarf 27

**C**
Carina Nebula 11
Cat's Eye Nebula 32–3, 34, 36
Centaurus constellation 22
Chandra space telescope 33
Chile 25
chromosphere 20
corona 20
Cosmic Microwave Background Radiation (CMBR) 60–1
Crab Nebula 38–9, 41
Crux constellation 24

**D**
diffraction spikes 22, 55
Dwarf Galaxy: UGC 8091 43

**E**
Earth 6, 14, 16, 20–1, 24, 29, 33, 38, 44, 49, 56–7, 58–9
Earth's atmosphere 7, 10, 13
electromagnetic spectrum 8–9, 10, 20
elliptical galaxy 42, 50
Euclid telescope 16
European Southern Observatory 25
Event Horizon Telescope 36

**G**
Gaia Space Observatory 56
Gaia Space Telescope 57
galactic bulge 57
gamma ray 9
GigaGalaxy Zoom project 44, 46–7
globular star cluster 30–1

gravity 20, 30, 32, 36
Great Barred Spiral Galaxy: NGC 1365 42

**H**
Helium gas 21
Horsehead Nebula 16–17
Hubble Space Telescope 7, 10–13, 17–19, 23, 31, 43, 47–8, 54–5
Hydrogen gas 15–16, 21, 29

**I**
infrared 8, 14–5, 29, 58–9
interstellar dust 45, 58
irregular galaxy 43

**J**
James Webb Telescope 5, 7, 10–11, 15, 27–8, 34–5, 38, 43
Jewel Box cluster 24–5
Jupiter 14, 16, 20, 22

**K**
Königsberg Observatory 6

**L**
La Silla Observatory 25
Leo constellation 52
Leo Triplet 52–3

**M**
M87 black hole 36
M87 galaxy 36
matter 8
Messier 15 30–1
microwaves 8
Milky Way 27, 44–6, 49, 50, 55, 56–7

**N**
N90 26
Near-Infrared Camera (NIRCam) 14
nebula 11–12, 14–17, 26, 32
NGC 602 26–7
NGC 1398 42
NGC 3627 53
NGC 3628 53

**O**
Orion Nebula 14–15
open star cluster 24, 26

Ophiuchus constellation 29
Orion constellation 14, 17

**P**
Pa 30 supernova 41
Pegasus constellation 30
Pillars of Creation 12–13
Pinwheel Galaxy 48–9
Planck Space Observatory, the 61
planetary nebula 32, 35, 36
photons 8–9
photosphere 21
Proxima Centauri 22–3
pulsar 38–9, 60–1

**R**
radiation 10, 20, 29, 32, 39, 58
radio waves 8
red dwarf 22
red giant star 32
Rho Ophiuchi 28–9
Russia 6

**S**
Sagittarius A* 45
Sculptor Galaxy: NGC 253 42
Small Magellanic Cloud 27
solar cycle 20–1
Solar Dynamics Observatory 20
solar eclipse 6
solar flare 20
solar prominences 20
solar system 20, 22
SOri62 16
Southern Ring Nebula 34–5
spiral galaxy 19, 42, 49, 53
Spiral Galaxy IC 2163 43

Spider Galaxy: UGC 5829 43
star 10–11, 13–15, 17, 20–2, 32, 36, 45, 50, 57
star clusters 10, 14, 19, 24
star formation 14, 16, 26–7, 29, 42, 49, 51
stellar nurseries 13, 24
Sun 6, 13, 20–2, 24, 29, 32, 34, 36, 41, 44, 57, 61
sunspots 21
supernova 36, 38, 41

**T**
Trapezium cluster 14
Two Micron All-Sky Survey (2MASS) 58–9

**U**
ultra deep field 54–5
ultraviolet 9, 11, 20
Universe 6, 7, 8, 10, 30, 54, 59, 60–1
Ursa Major 49

**V–Z**
visible light 8
William Herschel 24, 32
white dwarf star 32, 35, 41
Webb 34–5
William Anders 6

X-ray 9

zombie star 41

**Answers to the Quick quiz:**
1. c) Milky Way
2. c) Visible light
3. b) Infrared
4. c) A cloud of gas and dust
5. b) A star runs out of fuel and explodes
6. b) Ultraviolet
7. c) A region of space with gravity so strong nothing can escape
8. b) James Webb
9. b) Because each type of wave shows different things
10. c) To conduct an infrared survey across the whole sky